Contents

LIVING**ministry**

ABOUT THE AUTHOR

Dr Liz Graveling is part of the Church of England's National Ministry Team, where she leads the Living Ministry project and advises on research across the National Church Institutions.

Further information about Living Ministry can be found at
www.churchofengland.org/living-ministry

Church House Publishing
Church House
Great Smith Street
London
SW1P 3AZ

www.chpublishing.co.uk

Published 2020 for the National Ministry Team by Church House Publishing

ISBN 978 1 78140 213 9

We are grateful to all those who have given permission for us to share their stories. Please note that some names have been changed on request.

Scripture quotations are from the New Revised Standard Version of the Bible, Anglicized Edition, copyright © 1989, 1995 by the Division of Christian Education of the National Council of the Churches of Christ in the USA. Used by permission. All rights reserved.

The author and publisher are grateful to those who have allowed us to reproduce photographs in this booklet. Please note that none of the photographs included are of research participants.

A catalogue record for this book is available from the British Library

Concept and design by RF Design (UK) Limited

Printed in the UK by Ashford Colour Press

Foreword

Having multiple roles is a commonplace of clergy life. In writing this foreword, I wear at least three hats. I look back over thirty years of stipendiary ministry and see how far we have come in our understanding of clergy care and wellbeing.

I've also been leading the work which resulted in the Covenant for Clergy Care and Wellbeing. Grounded in a theology of care and self-care, this important national statement of intent is fed by a vast range of personal circumstances, needs and contexts that clergy face today.

Finally, as Chair of Trustees of Clergy Support Trust*, we are fortunate to have the resources to respond with generous financial help when someone's health or wellbeing faces a crisis. The Trust has begun to sponsor research and thought-leadership in the field.

I therefore have three reasons to welcome this resource and the quantitative and qualitative research that underpins it. It moves the Church 'from anecdote to evidence' and I hope it will equip all with responsibility in the field of clergy wellbeing to understand what is emerging from the Living Ministry project and what we can do together to promote the health and wellbeing of our ordained ministers.

Clergy Support Trust is delighted to sponsor this resource.

Canon Simon Butler
Senior Treasurer
Clergy Support Trust
Formerly known as the Sons & Friends of the Clergy

Introduction: Living ordained ministry

The glory of God is a human being fully alive.

St Irenaeus

'**As challenging and as bonkers as the whole thing is, to feel like you're doing something that every single part of you feels like you should be doing is the most amazing thing.**' So said a student preparing for a life of ordained ministry. But when and for whom do the challenges of ministry turn into unrelenting, crushing demands? How far does the sense of deep vocational fulfilment continue into the day-to-day life of ordained ministry? Amid the pressures and trials of daily life, how can clergy continue to flourish in their life with God and with other people?

Now, more than ever, in a church and a world turned upside-down by a global pandemic, such questions ring loud. These are some of the issues addressed by the Living Ministry project. Through statistical data from surveys and in-depth interviews and focus groups, we are following four cohorts of clergy (ordained in 2006, 2011 and 2015, and started training in 2016) over a period of ten years to understand what helps them to flourish in ministry. This booklet presents findings from the first wave of research, in 2017-18. It considers five interrelated aspects of wellbeing: financial and material; physical and mental; relationships; spiritual and vocational; and participation. With accompanying materials online, it is designed as a resource for dioceses, deaneries and individual ordained ministers, to support reflection on these areas as part of the 'big conversation' encouraged by the General Synod's 2020 Covenant for Clergy Care and Wellbeing. At the end, you will find a list of organisations providing support for wellbeing, some specifically for clergy and others more widely.

Throughout this booklet, years in brackets following quotations refer to the cohort to which the speaker belongs.

© KEITH BLUNDY / AEGIS ASSOCIATES

THE NATURE OF WELLBEING

Before looking in detail at specific aspects of wellbeing, let's consider the nature of wellbeing in general. The knowledge and experiences we have gathered from clergy themselves and from scholars working in this area reveal four characteristics of wellbeing that crosscut different areas of life.

Wellbeing is varied

In the 'quality of life' approach taken in this study, wellbeing is understood as subjective, in that different people have different ideas of what it means to be well. Moreover, while there are certain principles and practices of wellbeing that apply generally to the entire clergy population and beyond, experiences of ministerial life vary enormously. Socio-demographic differences, such as age, gender, family status, ethnic heritage and social class; ministerial differences, such as role, remuneration, ministry context, diocese and tradition; and circumstantial differences, such as finances, health and family situations, are all factors that influence the wellbeing of ordained ministers, along with changes over time.

Wellbeing is negotiated

Our lives are intrinsically bound up with the lives of those around us and the structures (social, economic, political, ecclesial and theological) with which we interact. Whether consciously or not, in everything from discussing a new role to applying for tax credits or deciding when and where to hold a standing committee meeting, clergy continuously negotiate their wellbeing with institutions, social forces and other people: family members, friends, colleagues, parishioners, senior clergy and diocesan officers, as well as government agencies and market forces.

Wellbeing is holistic

Because wellbeing is negotiated simultaneously across multiple arenas, clergy lives must be viewed holistically, understanding that changes in one area may have effects elsewhere. It is important to take a wide perspective and not draw hard lines between ministry and other aspects of life. Furthermore, wellbeing cannot simply be conflated with mental health: other aspects such as physical health, spiritual health, finances, relationships and vocation are important not only in how they affect mental health and each other, but also in their own right.

Wellbeing is a shared responsibility

Paradoxically, wellbeing itself – the pressure to be well – can sometimes feel like a burden. This is especially the case when the onus to maintain and improve wellbeing is placed entirely on the individual. Rather, and because of its negotiated nature, responsibility for wellbeing is shared between several parties, including family members, government and the church in all its guises (including local, deanery, diocese, national and theological education institution), as well as the clergyperson themselves, in providing and developing care for those who need it, resilience to handle the challenges of ordained ministry, and structures that help clergy flourish.

© KEITH BLUNDY / AEGIS ASSOCIATES

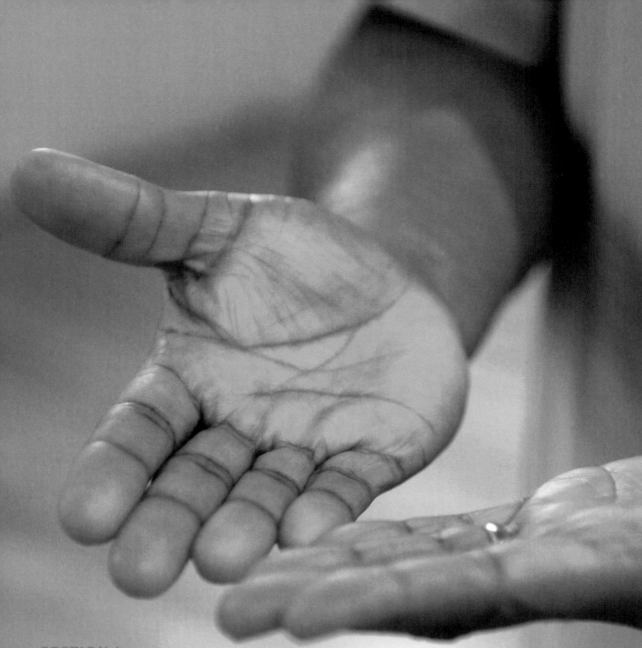

Spiritual and vocational wellbeing

Vocational clarity and fulfilment

Your eyes beheld my unformed substance. In your book were written all the days that were formed for me, when none of them as yet existed.

Psalm 139.16

Living Ministry participants reflect on their vocation at five levels.

1 CALLING TO PRIESTHOOD*

Having been ordained, some of the participants refer to a new sense of 'ontological rightness,' while others experience degrees of impostor syndrome. None feels they have made a fundamental mistake in discerning a vocation to ordained ministry; however, some raise questions about the specific nature of their calling and whether they can fulfil it. Sometimes one's original calling acts as an anchor during difficult times.

2 INSTITUTIONAL IDENTITY

A small number of participants voice doubts about whether they fit within the Church of England. Reasons vary, including exclusion through theological or social class differences and doubts about the possibility of fulfilling a specific calling; however, each mentions a perceived lack of care and understanding received from senior diocesan figures. An individual's sense of identity in relation to the church is affected by the way problems are addressed as much as the problems themselves.

3 SHAPE OF MINISTRY

More commonly, clergy reflect on the shape of their vocation within the church. An important factor contributing to vocational fulfilment is a sense that one's gifts, skills and passions are being used, including those acquired before ordination. Where this happens, clergy express deep vocational wellbeing. However, only two thirds of participants are satisfied that their current role utilises their training and capabilities, and lack of opportunity for this can lead to frustration. While some self-supporting ministers (SSMs) are able to integrate their 'secular' roles and their ministry, most discussion of bringing together previous experience and ordained stipendiary ministry is by curates and ordinands. Further waves of Living Ministry may reveal the extent to which these hopes are fulfilled. However, some clergy find vocational fulfilment in unexpected directions, when anticipated doors close and new ones open.

Diocesan vocational support is often centred on the Ministerial Development Review (MDR), which is a requirement for clergy under Common Tenure. MDR models vary between dioceses and, where participants find them helpful, much of the value is in facilitating the discernment and enabling of vocations. This works both as a tool for the minister to think through their own vocation and as a structure to provide input from senior clergy and permission to rest or release from anxiety. Underlying this, effective MDR can enhance a fundamental sense of being known, understood and valued.

66

SO I'M NOT WHERE I THOUGHT I WOULD BE. WOULD I CHANGE IT? ABSOLUTELY NOT.

Male chaplain, 2006

*None of participants in the qualitative study is pursuing a permanent vocation to the diaconate.

66

I'VE ALWAYS KNOWN ... THAT MY CALL IS TO THOSE TOUGH AREAS AND SMALL CHURCHES AND PLACES THAT AREN'T WELL RESOURCED. IT IS REALLY HARD WORK.

Male stipendiary minister, 2011

Where clergy question the helpfulness of MDR, it is largely because they do not experience it making any difference to their ministry and, where clergy feel misunderstood or ignored, the MDR can be damaging.

4 PLACES AND POSTS

While clergy articulate a deep vocation to ordained ministry, they can also feel strongly called to particular places and posts and, for many, this sense of calling is what sustains them during difficult times. This is not always straightforward, however. Some express doubts about whether they are in the right place. Reasons for this include: differences from the ministry context in theology or tradition, leaving clergy feeling unable to be themselves and uncertain of how accepted they are; insecurity of priest-in-charge roles; difficult church finances; unhelpful or uncaring congregations; responsibility for increasing numbers of churches through pastoral reorganisation; and shifting local or diocesan strategies which change the wider church landscape or require different ways of performing ministry. For others, thoughts about leaving their current role have less to do with problems than with the length of time they have been in post, recognising that a calling may be for a specific season. Still others believe themselves to be in the right place despite experiencing it as very hard.

5 TASKS OF MINISTRY

A further layer of calling is the tasks within a particular ministerial role. Clergy often find themselves engaged in work which they feel is outside their own personal calling, whether administrative or pastoral. While most recognise that less enjoyable elements of the job are inevitable and some frame them as part of their service and therefore calling, some experience such tasks as preventing them from fulfilling their vocation and challenging their spiritual wellbeing and identity as a priest. Three key factors appear to influence this:

» The extent to which the minister is obliged to engage in disagreeable tasks, which is partly determined by preferences about which tasks are dis/agreeable, as well as work boundaries and congregational participation.

» How far clergy are able to find some measure of vocational fulfilment outside their primary ministerial context. Ordained ministers may be engaged in a range of additional roles, including deanery, diocesan or cathedral roles, chaplaincy, or involvement with local community organisations. While some find these draining, for others they are life-giving in fulfilling a vocation that is not being met in one's main job; providing support and structure; or simply allowing a few hours away from the parish.

66

I DEFINITELY FEEL THAT I'M IN THE RIGHT PLACE, THE PLACE THAT GOD HAS CALLED ME TO AT THIS PARTICULAR MOMENT IN TIME. I THINK I'VE GOT THE SKILLS FOR THE JOB I'VE GOT ... I FEEL LIKE THE OTHER HALF OF MY LIFE HAS BEEN PREPARING ME FOR THIS HALF OF MY LIFE.

Male stipendiary minister, 2006

» Perceived levels of agency, i.e. the capacity to affect the situation. This does not necessarily correlate with seniority: while curates and assistant ministers often have limited power over the day-to-day shape of their ministry, they may find ways of managing, negotiating or exiting a difficult situation; incumbents have greater power within the parish, but are restricted by the burden of responsibility and the structures within which they work.

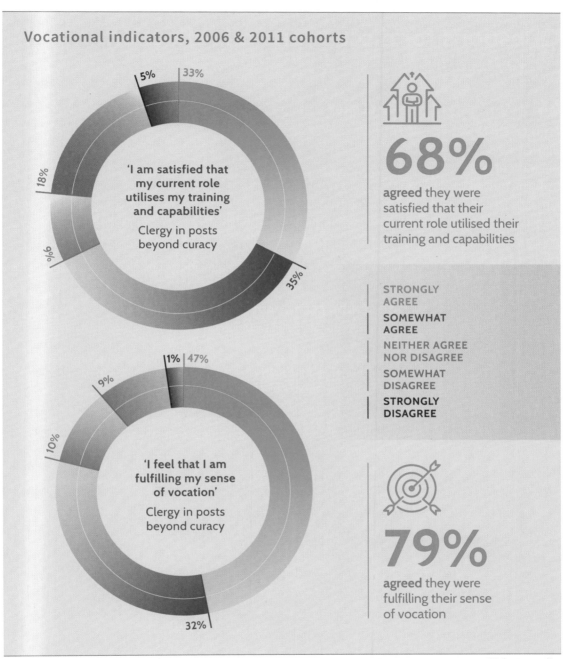

Vocational indicators, 2006 & 2011 cohorts

'I am satisfied that my current role utilises my training and capabilities'
Clergy in posts beyond curacy

33%
5%
18%
9%
35%

68% agreed they were satisfied that their current role utilised their training and capabilities

STRONGLY AGREE

SOMEWHAT AGREE

NEITHER AGREE NOR DISAGREE

SOMEWHAT DISAGREE

STRONGLY DISAGREE

'I feel that I am fulfilling my sense of vocation'
Clergy in posts beyond curacy

47%
1%
9%
10%
32%

79% agreed they were fulfilling their sense of vocation

Percentages may not sum to 100 due to rounding

INITIALLY THE CALLING TO DO THIS WAS VERY, VERY STRONG AND CONFIRMED BY VARIOUS SOURCES ... WHEN TIMES GET HARD I CAN ALWAYS GO BACK TO THAT STORY AND GO YES, I'M SUPPOSED TO BE DOING THIS.

Female stipendiary minister, 2006

Questions for discussion and reflection

MY DIOCESAN
BISHOP HAS
BEEN INCREDIBLY
SUPPORTIVE OF
ME. HE'S HELPED
ME IMMENSELY IN
MY TRAINING AND
EXPLORED ALL
SORTS OF THINGS
WITH ME.

Male stipendiary
minister, 2006

FOR CLERGY

1. Who is or can be a conversation partner in your ongoing vocational discernment?

2. How can you make the most of your Ministerial Development Review?

3. How does the balance of your ministry look? Have you got gifts/skills/ callings that are not being fulfilled? Are you feeling burdened by tasks you are not equipped to do? Does anyone in your diocese know?

4. Can you encourage yourself by reminding yourself of your original call?

FOR SENIOR CLERGY AND DIOCESAN OFFICERS

1. How do your clergy know that they and their ministry are valued?

2. Which of your clergy feel vocationally fulfilled regarding: ordained ministry; their role; their post; the tasks they are expected to do? What are acceptable levels of vocational dissonance?

3. Which of your clergy are not using their gifts and skills? How do your diocesan structures enable ongoing accompanied vocational discernment?

4. How effectively do you use Ministerial Development Reviews? Do you follow them up?

Spiritual wellbeing: strategies and resources

Vocational and spiritual wellbeing interact with other aspects of wellbeing. This includes stipendiary and self-supporting ministers understanding their vocation within the framework of remuneration and questioning their faith that God will provide during their retirement; clergy feeling spiritually as well as physically and mentally drained by their work and drawing on theology to identify appropriate boundaries; or clergy negotiating the shape of their ministry with family members and constantly attending to the spiritual welfare of others.

Spiritual wellbeing is affected by multiple issues (including workload, achievement, time, health, finances, personal circumstance and tradition); people (including family, friends, colleagues and those amongst whom one ministers); and structures (including local church, deanery, diocese, national church and other networks).

As with relational wellbeing, it is important that clergy find safe, non-judgemental spaces in which to talk and pray about their spiritual life. Strategies to attend to spiritual wellbeing fall into three broad categories (see below).

> ❝
> **WHAT WOULD WE DO WITHOUT WHATSAPP? YOU'VE ALWAYS GOT SOMEONE IF YOU NEED EMERGENCY PRAYER SUPPORT.**
>
> Female stipendiary minister, 2015

SELF-CARE
» Healthy daily, weekly, monthly and yearly rhythms of prayer, such as the daily offices, quiet days and retreats, often planned well in advance.
» Building prayer into regular routines, e.g. driving time, walks to and from school, dog-walking, running.
» Restorative retreats at times of crisis or low energy.
» Spiritual input and activity, e.g. books, conferences, sermon podcasts, music, poetry, writing, arts and crafts.
» Additional roles, e.g. chaplaincy, and identities, e.g. Franciscan.

SUPPORT FROM OTHERS
» Spiritual direction, mentors and critical friends.

» Peer support and prayer, including with immediate colleagues, in long-term cell groups or at ecumenical prayer meetings.
» Instant mutual support through media such as email, WhatsApp and Facebook groups.

STRUCTURAL SUPPORT
» Facilitated reflective practice groups or action learning sets.
» Pastoral supervision and counselling services, often provided by the diocese.
» Pastoral support from senior clergy.
» Permission-giving from senior clergy to spend time and money on spiritual self-care.

How beneficial were these support and development activities?

All clergy who took part in each activity

RETREATS
1
28%
71%

SPIRITUAL DIRECTION
3
30%
68%

ACADEMIC STUDY
6%
35%
59%

MENTORING OR COACHING
4
42%
54%

NETWORK CONFERENCES
3
46%
52%

LEADERSHIP DEVELOPMENT PROGRAMMES
7%
44%
50%

PEER-LED SMALL GROUPS
6%
40%
54%

ROLE-SPECIFIC DEVELOPMENT
6%
37%
57%

FACILITATED SMALL GROUPS
11%
34%
55%

MINISTERIAL DEVELOPMENT REVIEW
10%
32%
58%

DIOCESAN DAY COURSES
8%
27%
65%
1

IME PHASE 2 TRAINING
15%
26%
60%

OTHER
19%
82%
E.G. EXTERNAL TRAINING, PERSONAL STUDY

HIGHLY BENEFICIAL
MODERATELY BENEFICIAL
NOT BENEFICIAL

Percentages may not sum to 100 due to rounding

RESOURCING MY SPIRITUAL LIFE USED TO COME NATURALLY
TO ME AND WHEN I GOT INTO MINISTRY IT WAS LESS NATURAL.
YOU KNOW IT KIND OF FEELS LIKE I HAVE TO CONCENTRATE
ON IT BECAUSE EVERYTHING ELSE IS A DISTRACTION.

Female stipendiary minister, 2006

Personal and ministerial development

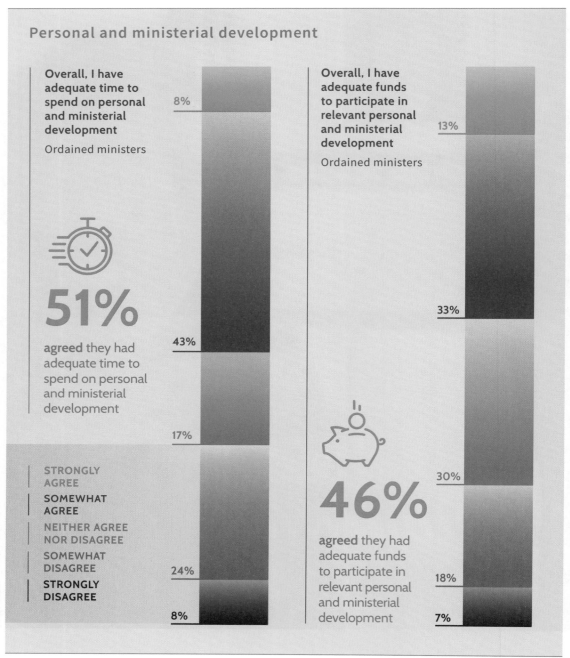

Overall, I have adequate time to spend on personal and ministerial development

Ordained ministers

8%

51%

agreed they had adequate time to spend on personal and ministerial development

43%

17%

| STRONGLY AGREE |
| SOMEWHAT AGREE |
| NEITHER AGREE NOR DISAGREE |
| SOMEWHAT DISAGREE |
| STRONGLY DISAGREE |

24%

8%

Overall, I have adequate funds to participate in relevant personal and ministerial development

Ordained ministers

13%

33%

46%

agreed they had adequate funds to participate in relevant personal and ministerial development

30%

18%

7%

Percentages may not sum to 100 due to rounding

IT CAN BE AN AWFUL BATTLE SUSTAINING ONE'S OWN SPIRITUAL RELATIONSHIP WHEN SO MUCH OF ONE'S SPIRITUALITY IS CONCERNED WITH OTHER PEOPLE'S SPIRITUALITY.

Female stipendiary minister, 2006

Questions for discussion and reflection

WHEN DO YOU GET
TIME TO SPEND
ALONE WITH GOD? ...
IT IS DIFFICULT AND
YOU HAVE TO BE
CREATIVE.

Male self-supporting
minister, 2015

FOR CLERGY

1. Who can you talk to on an ongoing basis about your spiritual development? Have you got a spiritual director?

2. Do you have healthy prayer rhythms in place? How can you build these up? Could you incorporate prayer more into your regular routines?

3. Where do you find spiritual nourishment? Can you draw on reading, sermon podcasts, conferences, creative arts, or worship or other spiritual activities outside your primary ministry context?

4. Do you take an annual (or more frequent) retreat?

5. Do you have spaces to talk and pray openly with other people?

FOR SENIOR CLERGY AND DIOCESAN OFFICERS

1. How do your clergy grow and mature spiritually? Are you aware of whether or not they are growing?

2. What kind of pastoral supervision do you provide for your clergy?

Physical and mental wellbeing

18

General health

**My grace is
sufficient for
you, for power
is made perfect
in weakness.**

2 Corinthians 12.9a

81%

of Living Ministry
participants
reported good or
excellent health

Overall, 81% of Living Ministry participants report good or excellent health.
A pattern emerges when analysed by current age, with younger ministers
faring better: across all cohorts, none of the under-32s report poor health
and nearly half experience excellent health, compared with 28% of those
aged between 32 and 54 and 24% of the over-55s reporting excellent health.

On the Warwick-Edinburgh Mental Wellbeing Scale, Living Ministry participants
score close to the average UK population, with married respondents reporting
slightly higher mental wellbeing than their single counterparts.

Along with other aspects of wellbeing, physical and mental health is
particularly vulnerable during transition periods, including entering training,
moving into curacy and then taking on and moving between roles of further
responsibility, each of which requires adapting to new roles and relationships,
often relinquishing previous support structures and, for many, uprooting to
a new location. The transition into first incumbency is often a moment of
particular stress, as clergy face first the pressure of securing a post before
their curacy stipend and housing run out, and then the new and sometimes
overwhelming responsibilities of incumbency.

**I DIDN'T EXPECT TO BE SO OVERWHELMED BY ALL OF THE ISSUES.
WHEN YOU ARE A CURATE YOU CAN JUST HAND THINGS OFF.**

Male stipendiary minister, 2011

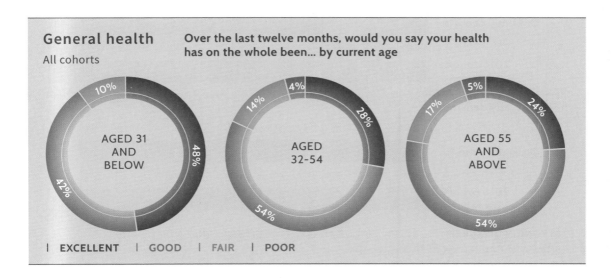

General health
All cohorts

**Over the last twelve months, would you say your health
has on the whole been... by current age**

AGED 31 AND BELOW — 10%, 48%, 42%

AGED 32-54 — 4%, 28%, 54%, 14%

AGED 55 AND ABOVE — 5%, 24%, 54%, 17%

| EXCELLENT | GOOD | FAIR | POOR

The demands of ministry

We asked ordinands and clergy how spiritually, emotionally, intellectually and physically demanding their ministry is. Ordinands report lower levels of spiritual, emotional and physical demand and higher levels of intellectual demand, consistent with the rigours of academic formation. However, they may overestimate the demands of their future ordained ministry.

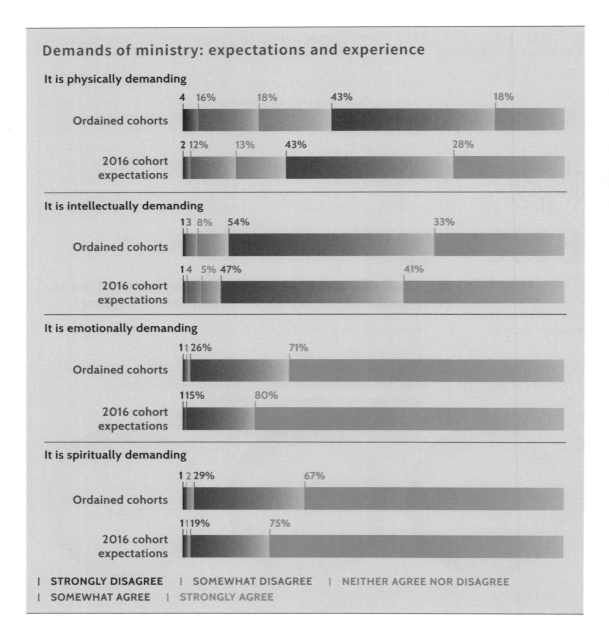

Demands of ministry: expectations and experience

It is physically demanding

Ordained cohorts: 4 | 16% | 18% | 43% | 18%

2016 cohort expectations: 2 | 12% | 13% | 43% | 28%

It is intellectually demanding

Ordained cohorts: 13 | 8% | 54% | 33%

2016 cohort expectations: 1 4 | 5% | 47% | 41%

It is emotionally demanding

Ordained cohorts: 11 | 26% | 71%

2016 cohort expectations: 11 | 5% | 80%

It is spiritually demanding

Ordained cohorts: 1 2 | 29% | 67%

2016 cohort expectations: 11 | 19% | 75%

| STRONGLY DISAGREE | SOMEWHAT DISAGREE | NEITHER AGREE NOR DISAGREE
| SOMEWHAT AGREE | STRONGLY AGREE

Questions for discussion and reflection

I DO CONTINUALLY
RECOGNISE THE
IMPOSSIBILITY OF
THE JOB AND HAVE
TO KEEP SAYING, OKAY
LORD, I CAN'T DO
EVERYTHING, WHAT
DO YOU WANT ME
TO FOCUS ON? ... IT'S
AN IMPOSSIBLE JOB
IF YOU TRY AND DO
EVERYTHING THAT
EVERYBODY EXPECTS.

Male stipendiary
minister, 2011

FOR CLERGY

1. Do you have healthy rhythms of work, rest, prayer and exercise? How could you build these up?

2. How well do you eat?

3. Are you aware of any provision by your diocese of counselling services?

4. Have you applied to charitable trusts such as St Luke's, Sheldon or the Clergy Support Trust for assistance with physical or mental healthcare?

5. Can you invest in building up your own resilience through reading and personal development courses?

6. From whom do you experience demands? Can you have honest conversations with these people about expectations? If not, could someone help facilitate such conversations?

7. Can you ration or delegate meetings?

8. Do you have a mentor or coach?

FOR SENIOR CLERGY AND DIOCESAN OFFICERS

1. Would you know if your clergy were facing challenges to their physical or mental health? How are they supported?

2. How can you help clergy to maintain healthy rhythms of work, rest and prayer? Do they feel they have permission to do so?

3. How are older clergy supported in their physical health?

4. What support is there for clergy approaching the end of their curacy?

5. What support is there for new incumbents? Are there sources of support lasting beyond the first few months (e.g. action learning sets and mentoring)?

Boundaries

MY CHAPLAINCY ROLE HAS BOUNDARIES TO IT, SO I KNOW WHERE I BEGIN THE WORKING DAY AND I END IT, I KNOW WHEN I'M ON CALL AND WHEN I'M NOT ON CALL.

Female self-supporting minister and chaplain, 2011

Boundaries, and the challenges associated with them, are key to understanding and managing many of the demands of ordained ministry. These include:

TEMPORAL BOUNDARIES

Many parish clergy use words like 'relentless,' 'overwhelming' and 'all-encompassing' to describe their workload. Although, under Common Tenure, full-time stipendiary clergy should receive 36 days of annual leave per year, including six Sundays, and should take a rest period of 24 consecutive hours every week, working hours are not defined in either quantity or time of day. However, this also allows for great flexibility, and none of the participants called for working hours to be defined. Those who have high workloads and low control over their diaries (such as training curates and some assistant ministers) find this aspect of ministerial demands especially challenging.

Chaplaincy often has more clearly defined temporal and spatial boundaries than parochial ministry, and some chaplains greatly appreciate the value of being able to leave work behind after a shift.

SPATIAL BOUNDARIES

Ordained ministry is rarely office-bound, and many vicarages are to some extent public as well as private spaces. Home becomes work through the physical presence of other people in the form of meetings, church offices and unplanned visitors; through people's virtual presence via telephone calls,

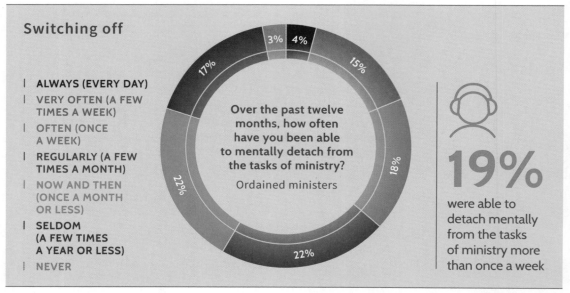

Switching off

Over the past twelve months, how often have you been able to mentally detach from the tasks of ministry?

Ordained ministers

3% 4% 15% 17% 18% 22% 22%

- ALWAYS (EVERY DAY)
- VERY OFTEN (A FEW TIMES A WEEK)
- OFTEN (ONCE A WEEK)
- REGULARLY (A FEW TIMES A MONTH)
- NOW AND THEN (ONCE A MONTH OR LESS)
- SELDOM (A FEW TIMES A YEAR OR LESS)
- NEVER

19% were able to detach mentally from the tasks of ministry more than once a week

Percentages may not sum to 100 due to rounding

> **WHERE DO I EVER STOP, BECAUSE I WORK FROM HOME? ... IT IS THAT BLURRING OF WHAT'S WORK AND WHAT'S HOME.**
>
> Female stipendiary minister, 2015

16%

reported feeling burned out from their role as a licensed minister a few times a month or more

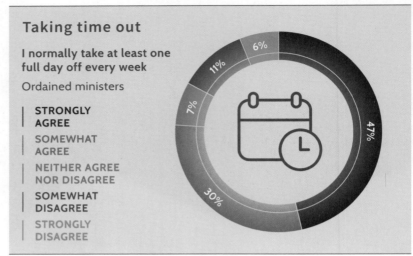

Taking time out

I normally take at least one full day off every week

Ordained ministers

- STRONGLY AGREE
- SOMEWHAT AGREE
- NEITHER AGREE NOR DISAGREE
- SOMEWHAT DISAGREE
- STRONGLY DISAGREE

6%
11%
7%
47%
30%

Percentages may not sum to 100 due to rounding

email and other media; and through other work-related activities that may be carried out at home, such as sermon-writing, service-planning and administration.

For the majority of stipendiary clergy who reside in their parish, living in the vicarage can feel like a 'goldfish bowl,' with clergy fielding comments from parishioners on everything from the state of their garden to the time they switch their light out at night.

MENTAL BOUNDARIES

Clergy often struggle to switch off mentally from their ministry, which can be compounded by the lack of temporal and spatial boundaries and increasing use of mobile technology.

Only 19% of respondents reported being able to detach mentally from the tasks of ministry more than once a week.

RELATIONAL BOUNDARIES

Clergy live in relationship with people both within and beyond their ministry, most obviously, for many, family members. The physical and mental wellbeing of either the ordained minister or their families can have a positive or detrimental effect on their relationships, and vice versa, sometimes with a spiralling effect.

ROLE BOUNDARIES

As with most jobs, clergy report enjoying some aspects of their role more than others. The tasks of ministry vary between person and context, with many clergy finding it difficult to share the burden of ministry with their congregations. Also draining is the unpredictable and fluid nature of ordained ministry, where clergy find themselves constantly switching between tasks that require very different skills and approaches.

I SOMETIMES FIND MYSELF COMPLETELY KNACKERED AND ABSOLUTELY WORN OUT BECAUSE I'VE BEEN DOING THINGS THAT I SHOULDN'T BE DOING, AND THEN FEELING LIKE A FAILURE BECAUSE I HAVEN'T GOT ANYBODY TO DO IT.

Male stipendiary minister, 2011

Managing ill-health

I WOULDN'T REALLY TRUST MY DIOCESE TO MAKE THEM AWARE THAT I HAVE A MENTAL HEALTH ISSUE.

Male stipendiary minister

All clergy sometimes have to manage sickness or injury, whether or not related to their ministry, and some enter ordained ministry with long-term conditions that affect their lifestyle and working practices. Conditions mentioned by participants include temporary injuries such as broken limbs, chronic physical and mental conditions, and age-related ill-health. Clergy may choose or feel obliged to manage ill-health themselves, usually in connection with their doctor but often without mentioning it to colleagues or senior clergy, either because they see it as their responsibility or because they lack trust in their diocese to support them appropriately. Most of those who describe seeking help, however, report being met with care and support. Especially important are the security of knowing practical cover will be provided at times of need, and personal acknowledgement and care from senior clergy.

47%

agreed that at a time of vulnerability they would access diocesan support (33% disagreed)

43%

agreed that their diocese offered adequate pastoral support for people like them (28% disagreed)

THE BISHOP WAS FANTASTIC, ABSOLUTELY WONDERFUL, HE EVEN CAME TO VISIT ME IN HOSPITAL ... WONDERFUL PASTORAL CARE, VERY THOUGHTFUL, VERY CARING.

Male chaplain, 2006

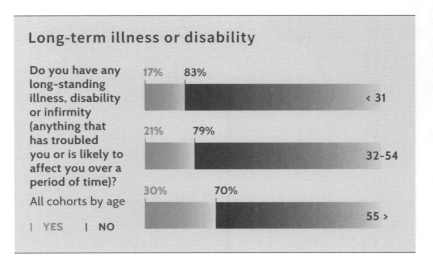

Long-term illness or disability

Do you have any long-standing illness, disability or infirmity (anything that has troubled you or is likely to affect you over a period of time)?

All cohorts by age

| YES | NO

17% 83% < 31
21% 79% 32-54
30% 70% 55 >

IT'S THE SHIFTING GEAR, THAT'S WHAT'S
EXHAUSTING, IT'S THE SHIFTING GEAR, BETWEEN
THAT PERSON WHO TURNS UP ON THE DOORSTEP
BECAUSE THEY DESPERATELY NEED TO TELL YOU
HOW FLAT THE EARTH IS, AND IT'S VERY URGENT
THAT THEY TELL YOU ABOUT IT NOW ... AND THEN
SHIFTING INTO OH I'VE GOT TO GO AND DO AN
ASSEMBLY, AND THEN SHIFTING INTO I'VE GOT
TO GO AND DO A FUNERAL.

Female stipendiary minister, 2011

Questions for discussion and reflection

THERE'S A HUGE
AMOUNT OF
FLEXIBILITY IF YOU
CAN GIVE YOURSELF
PERMISSION TO
DO THOSE THINGS.
THE FLEXIBILITY
IS THERE.

Female stipendiary
minister, 2011

FOR CLERGY

1. How can you ensure you have time and space away from work? Can you give yourself permission to rest? Whose permission do you need?

2. How flexible is your work? How can you maximise this?

3. How can you ensure you take an annual retreat?

4. Which of the following might be helpful?

   - Ringfencing days off, annual leave, time with family and friends, and other 'down time.'

   - Switching off your phone during rest times.

   - Using different phone numbers for work and personal life.

   - Getting away from the parish during rest times.

   - Moving meetings and the parish office out of your home.

   - Recording hours worked to relieve feelings of guilt.

   - Writing down work-related thoughts and concerns to 'park' them during rest times.

5. Who would you talk to if you were experiencing ill-health physically or mentally? Have you got support structures in place? If not, who can you talk to about this?

6. Do you know what provision there is in your diocese to support your physical and mental health?

FOR SENIOR CLERGY AND DIOCESAN OFFICERS

1. Are the clergy in your diocese given explicit permission to take time out for self-care and spiritual development? Are their parishioners aware of this?

2. Why might clergy in your diocese not access diocesan support at times of vulnerability? Are they encouraged to do so? How could pastoral support be improved?

SECTION 3

Relationship wellbeing

Isolation

I give you a new commandment, that you love one another.

John 13.34a

Ordained ministry is inextricably interwoven with other aspects of life and with other people's lives. It both affects and is affected by the interests, activities, needs and preferences of people close to the ordained minister. The relationships that hold these things together are not just instrumental, but in themselves a vital aspect of the wellbeing of clergy.

Ordained ministry can, however, be lonely work. Nearly a third of respondents feel isolated in their ministry, and a quarter feel isolated in their personal life. Respondents indicating the highest levels of isolation include: those in their first post after curacy; clergy aged 54 and under; men; those in full-time roles; incumbents; and those who are not married.

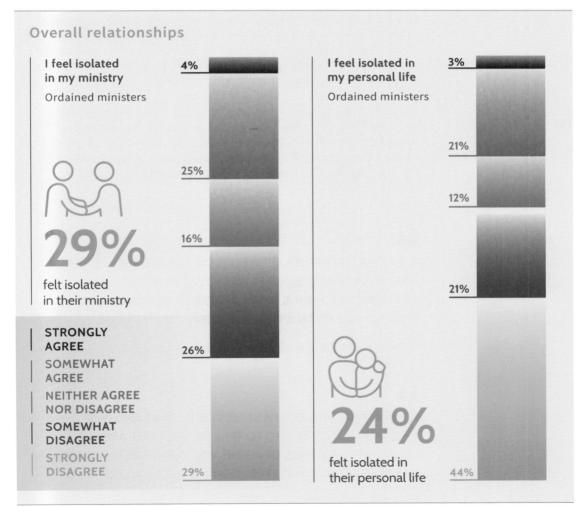

Overall relationships

I feel isolated in my ministry
Ordained ministers

4%
25%
16%

29%
felt isolated in their ministry

STRONGLY AGREE — 26%
SOMEWHAT AGREE
NEITHER AGREE NOR DISAGREE
SOMEWHAT DISAGREE
STRONGLY DISAGREE — 29%

I feel isolated in my personal life
Ordained ministers

3%
21%
12%
21%

24%
felt isolated in their personal life

44%

Percentages may not sum to 100 due to rounding

Family and friends

84%
found family
support highly
beneficial

Family and friends are the strongest sources of support, reported as highly beneficial to their flourishing in ministry by 84% and 65% of respondents respectively. However, these are also relationships that are likely to suffer due to the demands of ordained ministry. While workload is a major factor in this, with only 57% agreeing they had sufficient time to spend with their family, other aspects of ministry also contribute, including:

» Blurred boundaries between work and home, and public and private;
» Geographical constraints, with family needs or preferences regarding location and housing sometimes in tension with clergy role requirements;
» Financial concerns with limited stipends.

Ordained ministry is not, however, an immovable block around which everything else must fit. Rather, it is constantly negotiated as clergy seek to integrate work with family and other aspects of life. For some, this means limited options regarding working hours or location; for others, ring-fencing family time enables healthy work boundaries, or the flexibility of ministry allows parents to manage childcare responsibilities.

Wider family and friends are important as well as partners and children, but these relationships are even harder to maintain. While single clergy may be more deployable, they are also more likely to feel isolated, often having moved away from friends and family. Working six days a week, including evenings and weekends, makes it difficult to maintain relationships and support networks.

THERE'S A DIFFERENCE BETWEEN BEING SINGLE AND HAVING A FAMILY IN THAT IT'S QUITE EASY TO GET IN AT NIGHT AND TO CHEW OVER THINGS THAT HAVE GONE WRONG ENDLESSLY WITH NO ONE TO TALK TO ABOUT THEM.

Female stipendiary minister, 2006

I THINK THERE HAS BEEN A STRESS ON MY WIFE AND OUR CHILDREN. … THEY'VE HAD TO TAKE ALL THE GRIEF AND I'VE BEEN HAVING A WHALE OF A TIME, YOU KNOW, BECAUSE THIS HAS BEEN DOING WHAT I FEEL THAT I'VE BEEN CALLED TO DO.

Male stipendiary minister, 2011

Sources of support

Which sources of support have you found beneficial to your flourishing in ministry over the last two years?

Ordained ministers (where applicable)

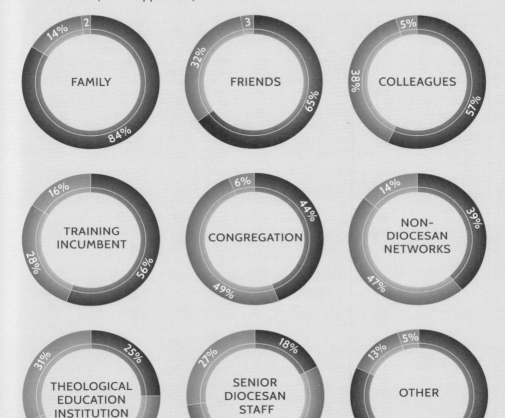

FAMILY — 14% · 2 · 84%

FRIENDS — 3 · 32% · 65%

COLLEAGUES — 5% · 38% · 57%

TRAINING INCUMBENT — 16% · 28% · 56%

CONGREGATION — 6% · 44% · 49%

NON-DIOCESAN NETWORKS — 14% · 39% · 47%

THEOLOGICAL EDUCATION INSTITUTION — 25% · 31% · 44%

SENIOR DIOCESAN STAFF — 18% · 27% · 55%

OTHER — 5% · 13% · 82%

| HIGHLY BENEFICIAL
| MODERATELY BENEFICIAL
| NOT BENEFICIAL

65%
found support from friends highly beneficial

56%
found support from their training incumbent highly beneficial

Percentages may not sum to 100 due to rounding

Questions for discussion and reflection

I FOUND EARLY ON NOBODY'S GOING TO RING ME TO SAY, 'HOW ARE YOU DOING?' ... SO I WENT OUT AND FOUND OTHER THINGS.

Male stipendiary minister, 2011

FOR CLERGY

1. Can you proactively build peer and diocesan relationships?

2. Can you ringfence time with people who care about you?

3. How does your ministry affect your family, and how does your family affect your ministry?

4. How much time do you spend with people unrelated to your work?

5. Can you give yourself permission to spend time with friends and family, not thinking about work?

6. If you are struggling to maintain friendships, can you identify a small number to invest in intentionally?

FOR SENIOR CLERGY AND DIOCESAN OFFICERS

1. Would you know if your clergy were feeling isolated? How often do you ask how they are?

2. How can you help single clergy to feel connected and supported?

3. Would you know if clergy were facing family challenges? What do you see as your responsibility to clergy families and how are they supported?

I'VE BECOME INCREDIBLY RUTHLESS WITH MY DIARY AS A WAY OF MAINTAINING MY FAMILY RELATIONSHIPS ... FAMILY HOLIDAYS ARE FIXED AND NON-NEGOTIABLE.

Female stipendiary minister, 2011

Congregations

EVEN THOUGH I'M ALWAYS ORDAINED, IF I'VE NOT GOT MY COLLAR ON I'M JUST NOW BEING MUMMY.

Female stipendiary minister, 2011

88%

felt generally supported by the people among whom they ministered

14%

agreed they would like to leave their congregation or place of ministry

Most clergy report positive relationships with those among whom they minister (for the most part, congregation members). The numbers conceal a range of expectations and experiences, relating to a variety of factors including role, circumstance and preference.

Self-supporting and ordained local ministers who remain part of the same parish when they are ordained face the challenge of managing the change in relationships that comes about through their new role. Many however, find fulfilment in integrating their priestly identity with their relationships with non-church work colleagues or their deeply rooted history in the local community.

Stipendiary ministers may also stay in one parish for long periods of time, but many move several times and may find it hard to put down roots. Relational boundaries with parishioners are complex, and the extent to which clergy build friendships in that context varies according to how they define friendship, how appropriate they consider such relationships to be and how able they are to build them. Some engage with parishioners at the level of social activity, although this may be intentionally limited because it blurs the boundaries of work and rest, and friendship and 'pastorship', and may also feed internal church politics. Others find practical or emotional support from their parishioners, or seek to share certain aspects of their lives, such as parenthood, while maintaining reserve about matters relating to ministry, sometimes using clerical dress to indicate which role is prioritised at any moment. Still others deliberately make themselves vulnerable and share personally in order to gain trust, although boundaries still tend to be set regarding the extent and depth of sharing.

As well as engaging through pastoral relationships and friendships, clergy also collaborate with parishioners in ministry. Experiences of this vary widely, with some clergy feeling misunderstood and criticised by members of their congregations and some struggling with low levels of participation, while others report high levels of support and engagement. Some describe having honest discussions with their congregations to express their limitations and manage expectations, although these can be difficult conversations and may be more helpfully facilitated externally.

I HAVE A LOT OF DIFFICULTY DETERMINING WHAT IS WORK AND WHAT IS FRIENDSHIP. ... SO, DAY OFF, SOMEBODY PHONES YOU, IS THAT WORK OR FRIENDSHIP IF THEY ARE IN TROUBLE? DO I SAY, 'TALK TO ME TOMORROW,' OR DO I SAY, 'I'LL DROP EVERYTHING AND SORT YOU OUT'?

Female ordained local minister, 2015

© KEITH BLUNDY / AEGIS ASSOCIATES

THERE ARE ASPECTS OF WHO I AM THAT I WOULD NOT SHARE
WITH PEOPLE IN THE PARISH, JUST TOO PERSONAL FOR THEM
TO KNOW ABOUT THEIR VICAR.

Male stipendiary minister, 2006

Colleagues

> **NOW, IN THE IMMEDIATE CONTEXT WITHIN THE PARISH, THERE IS NOBODY THAT I COULD REALLY SPEAK TO, ESPECIALLY ABOUT THE ISSUES OF PARISH LIFE.**
>
> Male stipendiary minister, 2011

81%

were satisfied overall with colleague relationships

74%

received sufficient support from people with whom they ministered

Overall, Living Ministry respondents report high quality relationships with colleagues. This, however, masks a great deal of variation between individual relationships: a clergy person may have excellent relationships with some colleagues and difficult relationships with others. Numerous factors contribute to the quality of each relationship, including: personality; socio-demographics (particularly noticed by those in minority or underrepresented groups, such as women, ethnic minorities, same-sex-attracted or working class clergy); context, with rural clergy, for example, sometimes working in remote parishes with few or no immediate colleagues; power dynamics, such as between curate and training incumbent; and proximity, such as differences between collegial relationships within the same church and within the wider deanery. Those working in chaplaincy commonly feel on the margins of the church, while self-supporting ministers working in parish ministry can also find themselves overlooked or under-esteemed, whether through implicit judgements about their capabilities or because clergy meetings do not fit with their other working hours. Relationships between incumbent and assistant minister and, especially, between curate and training incumbent, are complex, and clear expectations and communication are crucial.

Clergy interact with each other in multiple structured and unstructured ways, including deanery chapter; local ecumenical groups; action learning sets or other facilitated groups; training and development activities; prayer partners, triplets or cells; Facebook groups; WhatsApp groups; online huddles; and role-specific communities such as for pioneers. While relationships can be stressful as well as supportive, clergy often benefit from intentionally putting in place a range of support structures.

Relationships with other clergy are important in two key areas. First, positive relationships can provide support (practical, emotional or spiritual), including, crucially, a shared understanding of life as an ordained person and a safe space in which to speak openly without being judged. Second, they provide a way of locating oneself within the church (both Anglican and beyond). This may consist largely of networking and sharing information and good practice, but it can also contribute to shaping ministers' identities in relation to the church and their own vocation, strengthening or weakening a sense of belonging and interconnectedness.

> **I'M PART OF A FACEBOOK SUPPORT GROUP ... FOR ME THAT I THINK HAS BEEN A LIFE-SAVER ON MANY OCCASIONS.**
>
> Female stipendiary minister, 2006

© DIOCESE OF SOUTHWARK

WE'RE ALL CHAPLAINS AND WE UNDERSTAND ... IF I'VE BEEN
TO SOME PARTICULARLY DIFFICULT DEATH OR YOU KNOW,
A BABY WHO'S BEEN STILLBORN ... I KNOW I COULD TALK
TO ONE OF THE OTHER CHAPLAINS ABOUT IT.

Female chaplain, 2015

Questions for discussion and reflection

MY MINISTRY IS WHERE MY FEET ARE, TO A CERTAIN EXTENT, AND SO IF I SPEND TIME IN A PARISH, THAT'S WHERE IT IS, THE RELATIONSHIPS GET DEVELOPED, AND IF I SPEND TIME IN [WORK CONTEXTS], THAT'S WHERE MY MINISTRY IS DEVELOPED.

Male self-supporting minister, 2015

FOR CLERGY

1. Where do you place your relational boundaries with those amongst whom you minister? Do they understand the demands of your role and your personal limits?

2. Can you use team facilitation or personality profiling to build relationships in your parochial church council (PCC) or leadership team?

3. Is it helpful to remove your clerical collar when you are not formally on duty?

4. Where are your safe spaces? Who can you talk to openly and honestly?

5. Can you use private social media groups for support?

6. Are there networks of people in similar situations that you could join?

7. If you have a curate or a training incumbent, are you able to have honest conversations about expectations about role, workload, ministry style, working conditions etc.?

8. Are there tools and strategies you can draw on to help your 'team' work better together?

FOR SENIOR CLERGY AND DIOCESAN OFFICERS

1. What support is given to help clergy negotiate relationships within the parish? How is it different for incumbents, assistants/associates and clergy exercising sector, workplace or other ministries?

2. How many of your clergy have safe spaces in which to discuss personal or ministerial issues with people with whom they are not in a power relationship? How are these spaces found? How well do chapters work?

3. How well are curate/training incumbent expectations managed?

Financial and material wellbeing

Personal finances

Are not five sparrows sold for two pennies? Yet not one of them is forgotten in God's sight.

Luke 12.6

Financial and material wellbeing does not simply consist in achieving a certain absolute level of income or living standard. It is subjectively experienced relative to previous circumstances, friends and family, other clergy, and local standards of living (where clergy may be relatively wealthy or poor). Expectations are crucial. Levels of reported financial and material wellbeing are affected not only by the extent to which finances change on entering ordained ministry, but also by the extent to which clergy expect them to change and are reconciled to this. Those who maintain continuity with previous living standards experience the least impact on this aspect of wellbeing, while unforeseen events and circumstances can have serious financial implications.

Money carries symbolic as well as transactional value. While the stipend is designed to avoid placing monetary value on ministerial labour, stipendiary and self-supporting clergy may still measure the extent to which the church values them in terms of their financial remuneration, or lack of it, especially if value is not recognised and attributed in other ways.

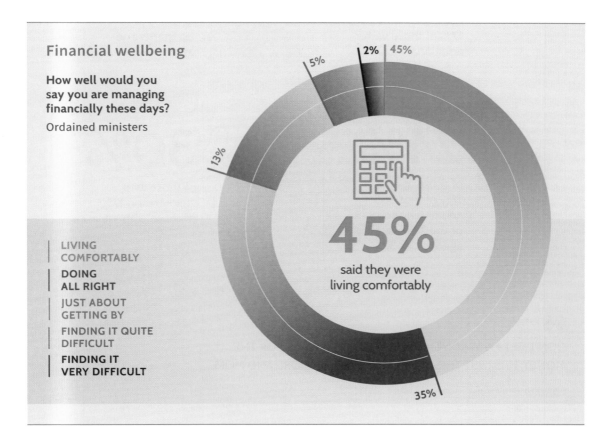

Financial wellbeing

How well would you say you are managing financially these days?

Ordained ministers

2% | 45%
5%
13%

LIVING COMFORTABLY
DOING ALL RIGHT
JUST ABOUT GETTING BY
FINDING IT QUITE DIFFICULT
FINDING IT VERY DIFFICULT

45%
said they were living comfortably

35%

The central factor associated with poor financial wellbeing is an absence of additional personal and/or household income to anything received in relation to ordained ministry.

81% of ordained respondents had additional income

Respondents who reported struggling financially:

33% of those without additional income, compared with **17%** of those with additional income

26% of incumbents, **18%** of curates and **11%** of assistants and associates

24% of those age 32-54, **17%** of those 55 and older, and none of the 26 respondents aged under 32

30% of those with children and **17%** of those without

"

DON'T GET ME WRONG, OF COURSE I'M NOT IN IT FOR THE MONEY. IT IS JUST THIS BEING ASKED TO DO MORE AND MORE.

Female ordained local minister, 2015

Housing

I LIVE IN A LOVELY HOUSE, IN A LOVELY VILLAGE ... BUT IT'S ENORMOUS AND IT COSTS ME AN ARM AND A LEG TO KEEP TO A TEMPERATURE.

Female stipendiary minister, 2006

61% of respondents live in tied housing, experiences of which vary enormously. Most commonly, clergy appreciate the size and relative value of their home but bemoan the high costs of heating and maintaining it, including sometimes paying for cleaners and gardeners to ease the pressure on time and energy. Tied accommodation provides some clergy with the opportunity to rent out other property, which in most cases provides a small net income.

Tied housing has implications beyond the financial. Vicarages are public as well as private spaces. Firstly, houses are only in the possession of the ordained minister for as long as they remain in post (and, for curates, not technically in their possession at all), contributing to a sense of dislocation and rootlessness.

Secondly, and as a consequence of this alongside the public nature of the ordained minister's role, vicarages are often partly used and occupied by parishioners as meeting, office or pastoral space. This has implications for finances (e.g. heating); for privacy (for clergy and their families); and for security (felt especially by single female clergy).

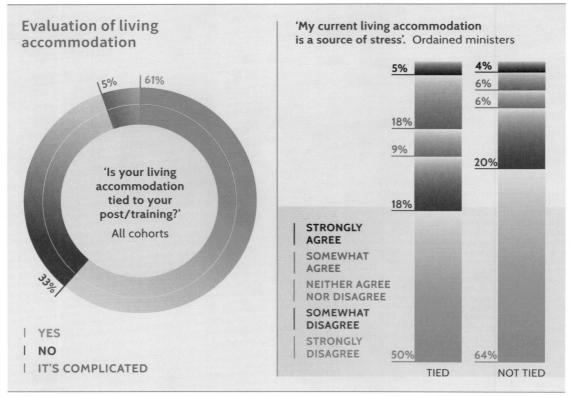

Evaluation of living accommodation

'Is your living accommodation tied to your post/training?' All cohorts

61%

5%

33%

- YES
- NO
- IT'S COMPLICATED

'My current living accommodation is a source of stress'. Ordained ministers

	TIED	NOT TIED
STRONGLY AGREE	5%	4%
SOMEWHAT AGREE	18%	6%
NEITHER AGREE NOR DISAGREE	9%	6%
SOMEWHAT DISAGREE	18%	20%
STRONGLY DISAGREE	50%	64%

Percentages may not sum to 100 due to rounding

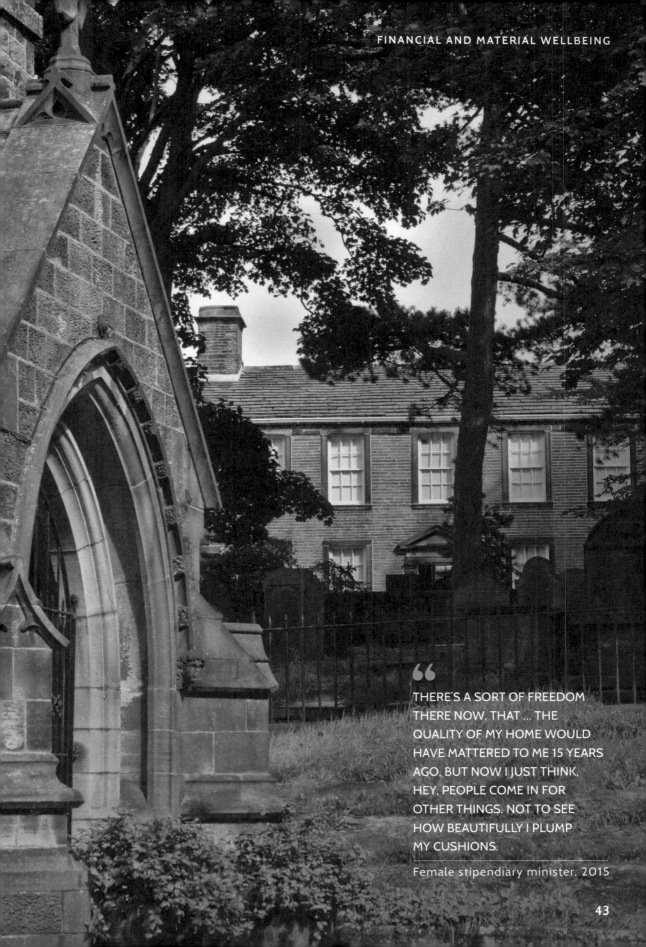

"

THERE'S A SORT OF FREEDOM THERE NOW, THAT ... THE QUALITY OF MY HOME WOULD HAVE MATTERED TO ME 15 YEARS AGO, BUT NOW I JUST THINK, HEY, PEOPLE COME IN FOR OTHER THINGS, NOT TO SEE HOW BEAUTIFULLY I PLUMP MY CUSHIONS.

Female stipendiary minister, 2015

Strategies and resources

Financial and material wellbeing is determined by diverse interrelating factors, such as socio-economic background, age, gender, family composition, household income, stage of ministry, role, remuneration, diocese, mode of training, context of ministry, housing costs, theology, government policy, lifestyle choices and personal circumstance. As well as their own interests, clergy negotiate and hold those of their families (nuclear and extended), involving both responsibility in providing and graciousness in receiving, in the context of close emotional relationships.

To maximise their wellbeing, clergy combine a range of resources and strategies, including: budgeting, savings, inheritance money, property, lodgers, charities, family assistance, additional household income, diocesan funds, credit cards, government benefits, insurance, expenses claims, dual or multiple roles, additional work or business, pensions and, of course, the stipend or salary.

Short-term and long-term savings

Please rate the following statements according to your current situation, by cohort

All ordained ministers

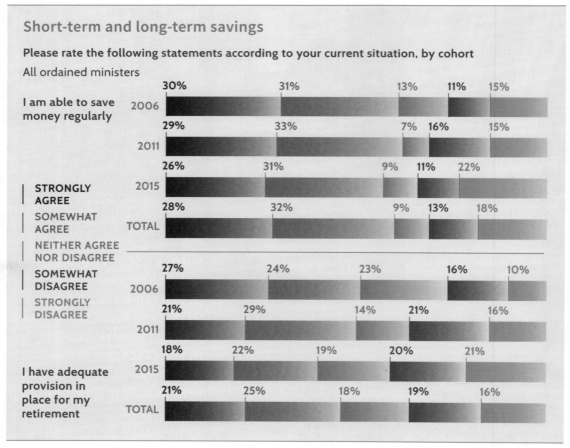

Percentages may not sum to 100 due to rounding

Parish finances

**I ALWAYS MAKE SURE
I TELL EVERYONE
ELSE TO MAKE SURE
THEY PUT THEIR
EXPENSES IN, BUT IT
IS DIFFERENT WHEN
YOU FEEL RESPONSIBLE
AND ARE TRYING
TO CUT CORNERS
IN EVERY PLACE YOU
CAN TO MAKE SURE
THINGS WORK.**

Male stipendiary
minister, 2011

Clergy in parochial roles have to negotiate financial boundaries with their parish, usually expressed through claiming expenses and giving to the church. The distinction between personal and ministry expense is not always clear, and parishes can have very different expectations of what their clergy are entitled to (e.g. travel, retreats, events and resources).

The way participants position themselves in discussions about expenses varies by cohort, reflecting perceptions of power and responsibility. Thus, most of the curates discuss expenses in terms of what the church will allow them to claim for. On the other hand, incumbents are more likely to frame discussions about claiming expenses in terms of their own decision-making, sometimes influenced by the state of the church's finances. Giving and expenses are interrelated, where not claiming expenses is a form of giving to the church, and several incumbents express a feeling of personal responsibility towards their church's financial situation, actively expressed through decisions both to give financially to the church and not to claim expenses, as well as, in some cases, personally funding church-related costs such as administrators' wages. Awareness that the stipend is funded at least in part through congregational contributions to parish share can heighten the sense of responsibility.

**WHEN I MOVE, [MY CHURCH] WILL LOSE MY PLANNED GIVING. …
I AM THE BIGGEST GIVER IN THE CHURCH … AND THAT'S GOING
TO HAVE A DRASTIC EFFECT ON THEM. … PARTICULARLY WHEN
YOU ARE THE INCUMBENT IN A STIPENDIARY POSITION YOU ARE
ALWAYS AWARE OF THE BURDEN THAT IT IS UPON THE CHURCHES.**

Female stipendiary minister, 2006

THE PARISH SAYS, 'GO TO YOUR
SPIRITUAL DIRECTOR, GO ON RETREAT'
AND I SAY, 'WELL ARE YOU GOING TO
HELP WITH THE FUNDING OF THAT?' 'NO.'

Female self-supporting minister, 2015

I'VE GOT ... PARISHES THAT
PAY MY EXPENSES WITHOUT
ASKING QUESTIONS.

Male stipendiary minister, 2015

Questions for discussion and reflection

YOU MAKE YOUR
HOME IN THE PLACE
THAT YOU LIVE IN,
WHICH IS NOT THE
SAME AS LIVING IN
YOUR OWN HOME.

Female stipendiary
minister, 2011

FOR CLERGY

1. How easy is it to make ends meet each month?

2. What would you do in a financial crisis?

3. Are you able to save regularly?

4. Do you budget? Could this help?

5. Do you know what provision you have for retirement? Can you do anything more to plan for this?

6. Do you know who to talk to about housing issues, financial matters and retirement plans?

7. Have you explored potential sources of financial support (e.g. diocesan, trusts, government)?

8. Do you always claim expenses? If you are in parish ministry, how easy do you find it to draw boundaries between your own finances and those of your church?

FOR SENIOR CLERGY AND DIOCESAN OFFICERS

1. How well does tied housing work in your diocese? Is it an expression of care or a source of stress for clergy?

2. Are you aware of clergy struggling to make ends meet? If not, is that because they're fine or they hide it? If so, what kind of support do you provide? Do you know which clergy are most at risk?

3. Do clergy feel valued? What can you do to ensure they do?

4. How many of your clergy are approaching retirement? How many worry about this? What support is there for clergy approaching or needing to plan for retirement?

5. How far do clergy feel responsible for parish finances? Who can they turn to?

Participation wellbeing

National and diocesan discourses

We, who are many, are one body in Christ, and individually we are members one of another.

Romans 12.5

THE IMPORTANCE OF TOP COVER, THE SENSE OF SOMEONE EXTERNALLY SAYING 'YOU ARE OKAY, YOU ARE DOING OKAY. I APPROVE OF WHAT YOU ARE UP TO AND I SUPPORT YOU.'

Male stipendiary minister, 2006

The factors that influence the ability of clergy to participate as they would like in the life of the wider church are many and varied. Clergy participate in the life of the church in diverse ways, at deanery, diocesan and national levels as well as through networks outside formal church structures.

While some have felt more connected to the national church in recent years, through increased investment in national communications, there is also a sense among some of disconnect from the dominant values and strategies conveyed by the National Church Institutions and Archbishops. Parish clergy feel the twin pressures to demonstrate rising attendance figures and to meet their parish share in full, and are demoralised when they do not achieve either of these (although a supportive parish share system can lead to an increased sense of connectedness and a deeper desire to support others when they can afford it). At the same time, they are aware of huge sums of money being invested in other growth strategies, notably resource churches. For some, this results in vocational alienation, where one's approach and identity as a priest in the Church of England is threatened. For others, ministering in places distant from the foci of investment, the alienation is contextual. Still others, who may be aligned with the general growth strategy and working hard to achieve it, feel devalued and marginalised in terms of resources.

Alongside this, significant value is placed by clergy on personal recognition from senior clergy, in relation to both their ministry and their personal lives. Clergy greatly appreciate pastoral care, practical assistance and proactive contact from their bishop(s) in particular: underlying this is the importance of being and feeling known, understood, cared for, supported, affirmed and, above all, valued.

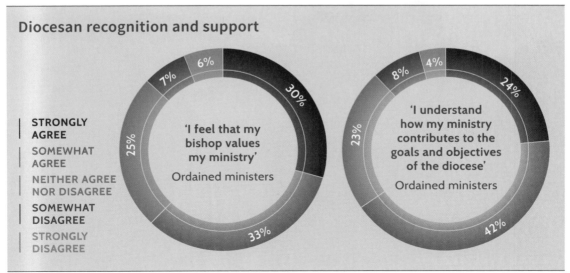

Diocesan recognition and support

STRONGLY AGREE
SOMEWHAT AGREE
NEITHER AGREE NOR DISAGREE
SOMEWHAT DISAGREE
STRONGLY DISAGREE

'I feel that my bishop values my ministry'
Ordained ministers

7% | 6% | 30% | 33% | 25%

'I understand how my ministry contributes to the goals and objectives of the diocese'
Ordained ministers

8% | 4% | 24% | 42% | 23%

Percentages may not sum to 100 due to rounding

Social, theological and structural difference

ATTENDING A
COLLEGE OF
A DIFFERENT
TRADITION HAS
MADE ME A MUCH
MORE ROUNDED
MINISTER IN THE
CHURCH. ... THAT
WAS WONDERFUL.

Female stipendiary
minister, 2015

The ability for clergy to participate in the life of the wider church varies greatly. Sometimes this is influenced by personal preference or circumstance; however, certain groups experience exclusion and marginalisation more than others. These include:

» Self-supporting clergy and those in sector ministry, who sometimes feel on the margins of deanery and diocesan life. They may be restricted in capacity to participate in meetings because some or all of their professional time is paid for by other organisations, or they may feel they are treated as a lower class of priest, either in personal relationships or through administrative systems.

» Same-sex-attracted clergy, who experience practical and emotional stress from living and ministering within a church that is not reconciled to their sexual identity. This may include exclusion by other clergy; restricted job options; and discomfort with the high level of attention given to this one aspect of their identity.

» Clergy who feel they do not fit the culture of the Church of England in terms of social class or education. Some describe feeling marginalised or looked down on by senior clergy and peers because of their 'ordinary' or non-academic background.

© KEITH BLUNDY / AEGIS ASSOCIATES

THE OTHER CHURCH
IS VERY HIGH, AND WE
ARE LOW EVANGELICAL
… ALTHOUGH I KIND OF
HANG AROUND ON THE
EDGE OF THEIR GROUP,
IT'S STILL A GROUP
WHICH I THINK, 'WELL,
I'M NOT REALLY PART
OF THIS.'

Female stipendiary
minister, 2006

» Clergy ministering in an environment where the majority are of a different tradition. This may be at diocesan level, at deanery or benefice level, or within one's parish(es). Clergy who are part of theological minorities (e.g. traditional Anglo-Catholics and conservative Evangelicals) may also feel marginalised and struggle to find posts. Some clergy, however, experience contrasting perspectives and practices as helpful in broadening their spirituality and understanding of other traditions.

» Female clergy, who remain disadvantaged in multiple ways despite formal acceptance within all orders of ministry in the context of mutual flourishing and the Five Guiding Principles. Depending on their circumstances, women are still more likely than men to encounter restrictions such as childcare responsibilities, limited working hours, geographical immobility, lack of understanding by colleagues and silent or explicit rejection of their vocational legitimacy. They may also have to work through their own internalised gendered attitudes and, because they represent disproportionately high numbers of older and self-supporting clergy, they are more affected than men by the barriers faced by these groups as well as the advantages.

Some other aspects of social difference, particularly ethnicity and disability, were notable for their near absence in the accounts of Living Ministry participants, reflecting the lack of diversity or possible unwillingness to share experiences in these areas.

"

I DIDN'T HAVE A
CHURCH BACKGROUND
AND I DIDN'T
UNDERSTAND A LOT
OF THE THINGS THAT
GO ON IN CHURCHES
WHICH I THINK ARE
NATURAL TO PEOPLE
WHO ARE SORT OF
CHURCH FROM BIRTH.

Female self-supporting
minister

Questions for discussion and reflection

I WENT TO MY FIRST
CHAPTER MEETING
IN 8 YEARS, LAST
MONTH, BECAUSE
THEY MOVED IT
TO A TIME WHEN
I COULD GET TO IT:
THEY MOVED IT
TO A BREAKFAST.

Male self-supporting
minister, 2006

FOR CLERGY

1. Can you be proactive about building relationships with peers, senior clergy and diocesan officers?

2. If you are feeling under pressure regarding attendance and finance, you are not alone. Who can you talk to about this?

3. How are people included or excluded in your deanery or diocese?

4. Are there things you can change to be more inclusive, e.g. rotating the times and locations of meetings?

FOR SENIOR CLERGY AND DIOCESAN OFFICERS

1. How far do clergy in your diocese feel under pressure to pay parish share and increase attendance figures? How does this impact their wellbeing?

2. Does diocesan strategy always take into account clergy wellbeing? What messages do clergy receive from the diocese about mission and ministry?

3. How much contact do clergy have with their bishop? Do they know that they are known, understood and valued?

4. Have you considered the specific experiences and barriers in your diocese to: female clergy; same-sex attracted clergy; clergy not from highly educated, middle class backgrounds; clergy from ethnic minorities; clergy with disabilities, clergy from theological minorities or working in traditions different from their own? How can you support these groups?

Six Ways Clergy Thrive

I came that they may have life, and have it abundantly.

John 10.10b

From the stories of our participants, seen through the lens of these five aspects of wellbeing, have emerged six key things that make a difference to clergy wellbeing.

This is not a magic formula; rather, six principles that have consistently contributed to wellbeing across varying people, roles and circumstances.

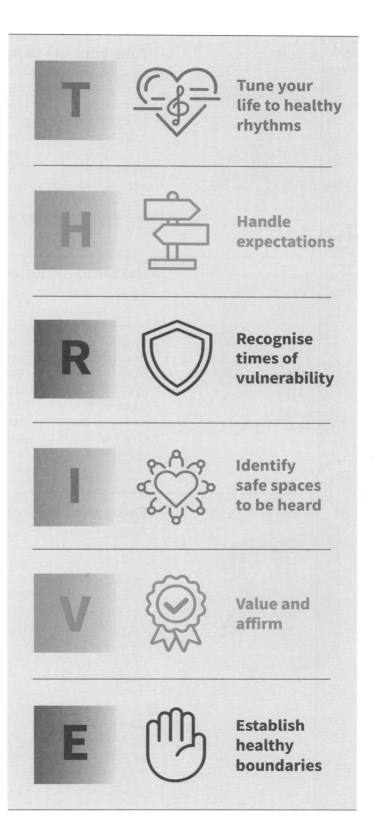

T — Tune your life to healthy rhythms

H — Handle expectations

R — Recognise times of vulnerability

I — Identify safe spaces to be heard

V — Value and affirm

E — Establish healthy boundaries

Tune your life to healthy rhythms

The unbounded nature of much ordained ministry, along with the immense variety of clergy lives and contexts means that structured routines can be elusive. To maintain wellbeing and flourish in ministry, clergy often develop their own life-giving rhythms of work, rest, prayer, exercise and nutrition. These may involve a combination of adapting existing routines such as travel and dog-walking, and designating specific time to particular activities. They may be daily, weekly, monthly or yearly patterns – or any other frequency – and will be more or less fluid and flexible depending on activity and context.

Handle expectations

One of the most common causes of stress in all aspects of wellbeing is unclear expectations. This may be about specific mis-matched expectations such as in the context of a new relationship between training incumbent and curate, a clergy family navigating the expectations of congregations, or tensions between a vicar and her PCC over expense claims, or it may relate to differences between anticipated and actual experiences of ordained ministry or particular roles, whether financial, vocational, relational, physical, mental or spiritual. Clear communication is important, both the capacity to express one's own limits and perspectives and the capacity to hear others.

Recognise times of vulnerability

Along the journey of ordained ministry there are certain times when clergy will be more vulnerable to dips in wellbeing. It is important to recognise such moments, both to put in place preventative strategies and support structures and to maintain perspective. Moments of transition are especially challenging, in particular the move from curacy to first incumbency. First incumbents describe feeling isolated and overwhelmed by level and scope of responsibility, mitigated for some by mentors, proactive and approachable archdeacons, and training for new incumbents. Wellbeing is also threatened at moments of personal or ministerial crisis, whether a health issue, family bereavement, financial or congregational difficulty or a global pandemic, and both personal resilience and diocesan support are important at such times. The latter varies, partly according to whether help is sought (and whether the minister feels they can seek help), and may include financial assistance, counselling provision, professional cover, advice, guidance and pastoral care.

Identify safe spaces to be heard

Partly because of the challenges of relational boundaries in pastoral ministry, ordained ministers often have to look beyond their immediate context in the search for authenticity. Safe, honest and supportive relationships are often (not always) found in other clergy, whether individuals, longstanding peer groups, diocesan-initiated reflective practice groups or networks of people in similar circumstances. They may meet on a regular basis for deep sharing and prayer, or communicate via social media for instant support, and often combine both. Groups built into ecclesial structures, such as deanery chapter, may or may not provide such support, and clergy also draw on spiritual direction, mentors and counsellors as well as family and friends.

Value and affirm

Of utmost importance is the need to be recognised and valued at a human level as well as by God. In the context of a declining church and pressure to increase attendance and ensure financial viability, alongside huge financial investment in specific initiatives, clergy can feel unappreciated, devalued and demoralised. The implications of this cut across all aspects of wellbeing, from the perceived need to reduce personal expenditure to support a struggling church, to physical and mental stress, isolation, guilt, vocational doubt and a strong sense of marginalisation. Awareness of the implications of dominant messages from the church for clergy wellbeing is important, and where clergy receive personal interest in and support of themselves and their ministry, especially by senior clergy, they feel less guilty and isolated, and more known, understood and valued.

Establish healthy boundaries

Ordained ministry has few formal borders. Clergy, especially those in parish ministry, struggle with work that impinges on family time, intrudes into private space, invades rest and sleep, complicates relationships, inhibits expense claims and expands into all the minutiae of church life. To address this, as well as nurturing healthy rhythms of living, many clergy also seek to develop life-giving boundaries in time, space, mind, role, relationships and finances. Diocesan support in this is vital in providing guidance, examples, validation and permission, to nurture an environment in which clergy are able to be kind to themselves as well as to others.

Questions for discussion and reflection

1. As you have read this booklet, what has struck you most about clergy wellbeing? What troubles you?

2. How has the Covid-19 pandemic changed your personal, ministerial and diocesan practices and affected your wellbeing and that of the clergy in your diocese?

3. Where do you think you are doing and feeling well at the moment, and what are you finding challenging?

4. Which things could be impacted by a small, doable change, which is it hard to know how to tackle, and which would require significant cultural or structural change?

5. What changes can you make and what must be left to others?

6. What practical steps will you take to follow this up?

7. Who can you talk about it with?

Methodology

Living Ministry is a longitudinal research project conducted by the Church of England's National Ministry Team to understand what helps clergy flourish in ministry. Every two years, we invite everyone ordained in 2006, 2011 and 2015, and who started training in 2016, to respond to an online statistical survey, followed a few months later by interviews and focus groups with a smaller sample. This booklet draws on data from Wave 1, during which 761 ordinands and clergy from all dioceses took part in the survey, with 85 going on to participate in the qualitative study.

Because Living Ministry is a cohort study and because no one is obliged to take part, it is not representative of all clergy. For example, the proportions of women and younger clergy who have participated are higher than those of the entire clergy population, reflecting the fact that the cohorts we are working with have all been ordained since the relatively recent year of 2006.

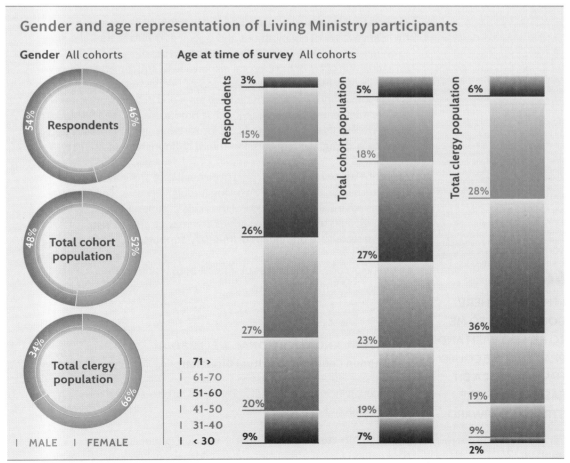

Gender and age representation of Living Ministry participants

Gender All cohorts

- Respondents: 54% / 46%
- Total cohort population: 48% / 52%
- Total clergy population: 34% / 66%

| MALE | FEMALE

Age at time of survey All cohorts

| | 71 >
| | 61-70
| | 51-60
| | 41-50
| | 31-40
| | < 30

Respondents: 3%, 15%, 26%, 27%, 20%, 9%

Total cohort population: 5%, 18%, 27%, 23%, 19%, 7%

Total clergy population: 6%, 28%, 36%, 19%, 9%, 2%

Percentages may not sum to 100 due to rounding

Resources

Accompanying resources to this booklet, along with the detailed Living Ministry reports, can be found at www.churchofengland.org/living-ministry:

» Wave 1 quantitative report (2017):
Mapping the Wellbeing of Church of England Clergy and Ordinands

» Wave 1 qualitative report (2018):
Negotiating Wellbeing: Experiences of Ordinands and Clergy in the Church of England

» Wave 2 quantitative report (2019):
Ministerial Effectiveness and Wellbeing: Exploring the Flourishing of Clergy and Ordinands

Beyond the responsibility clergy and ordinands hold for their own self-care, there are a range of organisations and resources on which they can draw to enhance their wellbeing. While support from the diocesan bishop is an expression of his or her pastoral responsibility, structures vary from diocese to diocese. In some dioceses and cathedrals, wellbeing falls under the responsibility of a multi-disciplinary team and in others responsibility is more fragmented. Some dioceses have produced their own resources for clergy wellbeing, such as the Oxford Diocese Flourishing in Ministry booklet. www.oxford.anglican.org/mission-ministry/flourishing-in-ministry

Anglican Pastoral Care are advisers in pastoral care and counselling in the Church of England, usually working through dioceses. Their website contains advice and an overview of the kinds of support available, along with links to other organisations that may be able to help. http://pastoralcare.org.uk/about/ministry-support/

Listed below are some sources of support both inside and outside the Church of England.

> ## 66
> I THINK I'M WHERE GOD HAS ASKED ME TO BE. I DO WISH AND PRAY THAT HE COULD HAVE MADE IT A BIT EASIER AND MORE STRAIGHTFORWARD.
>
> Female self-supporting minister, 2011

SPIRITUAL AND VOCATIONAL WELLBEING

The **London Centre for Spiritual Direction** offers resources and support for all those interested in Christian spiritual direction or exploring their faith formation. It includes a directory of spiritual directors across the country. www.lcsd.org.uk

Spiritual Directors International is an inclusive, global learning community of people from many faiths and many nations who share

> MY CALLING TO THIS CHURCH WAS VERY STRONG TO START WITH, BUT IT'S SOMETHING I'M BEGINNING TO QUESTION. ... I WILL DO WHATEVER I'M ASKED TO DO, WHETHER THAT'S STAY OR MOVE OR WHATEVER.

Female stipendiary minister, 2006

a common passion and commitment to the art and contemplative practice of spiritual direction. Includes directories of retreat centres and spiritual directors.
www.sdiworld.org/find-a-spiritual-director

The **Retreat Association** is a national Christian organisation set up to help people find ways of exploring and deepening their journey with God through spirituality and prayer. Their website includes information about retreat houses and programmes, spiritual direction, events, training and other resources.
www.retreats.org.uk/index.php

The **Sheldon Hub** is for clergy, ordinands and others in ministry, offering an independent supportive online community, a live directory of people and places, and a bank of trustworthy advice covering most areas of wellbeing.
www.sheldonhub.org/

PHYSICAL AND MENTAL WELLBEING

St Luke's supports the physical and mental health of Anglican clergy and ordinands, working through dioceses and directly with individuals, and providing online information and resources about wellbeing.
www.stlukesforclergy.org.uk/

The **Society of Mary and Martha at Sheldon**
is a community and retreat house specialising in supporting people in Christian ministry. See also the Sheldon Hub, in the spiritual & vocational wellbeing section above.
www.sheldon.uk.com/

Every Mind Matters is an NHS resource that provides expert advice and practical tips to help you look after your mental health and wellbeing.
www.nhs.uk/oneyou/every-mind-matters/

Mindful Employer provides guidance and signposting for individuals to maintain their own wellbeing and where to go when in need of extra support, as well as resources on how to be a good employer by supporting the mental wellbeing of staff.
www.mindfulemployer.net

Mind advises and supports anyone experiencing a mental health problem, through information and signposting, local support and care, networks and membership, campaigning, and training.
www.mind.org.uk/

The **Mind and Soul Foundation** aims to bridge the gap between mental health and Christian spirituality through sharing the best of Christian theology and scientific advances; helping people meet with God and recover from emotional distress; and engaging with the local church and mental health services.
www.mindandsoulfoundation.org/

MY FRIENDS LIVE
ALL AROUND THE
COUNTRY AND I FIND
IT REALLY SUPPORTIVE
BEING ABLE TO GET IN
TOUCH WITH PEOPLE
VIA SOCIAL MEDIA
PRIVATELY. THAT'S
WHERE I GET A LOT
OF SUPPORT.

Male stipendiary
minister, 2015

RELATIONSHIPS

Bridge Builders provides training and shares resources and ideas to support church leaders and congregations in the challenging task of living as models of reconciliation.
www.bbministries.org.uk/

The Family Mediation Council provides information about suitable local mediation services, as well as offering mediation itself.
www.familymediationcouncil.org.uk/

Broken Rites supports clergy spouses/partners who are experiencing difficulty in their relationships, including providing practical information, one-to-one support, group meetings and a facebook group.
www.facebook.com/BrokenRites/ http://brokenrites.org/

Lawworks is a charity offering legal advice to those who are not eligible for legal aid and cannot afford to pay.
www.lawworks.org.uk/

There are various Facebook groups to support clergy, including **Clergy Mummies, Clergy Spice** (for spouses of clergy), **Clergy Family Network, Curates in Training** and **Female Ordinands and Curates**.

FINANCIAL AND MATERIAL WELLBEING

The Clergy Support Trust aims to promote and sustain the wellbeing of Anglican clergy and their dependants. One of the ways it does this is through providing financial grants to households experiencing hardship or other need. Eligible beneficiaries include members of the clergy, ordinands and the spouses, former spouses, children and dependants of living or deceased members or former members of the clergy or ordinands.
www.clergysupport.org.uk/

The **English Clergy Association** provides holiday grants in order to give clergy and their families a rest from duty and contribute to their enjoyment of human life.
www.clergyassoc.co.uk/content/home.htm

The **Cleaver Ordination Candidates Fund** supports Anglican ordinands committed to a traditional Catholic understanding of the priesthood and episcopate and offers grants to support candidates exploring a vocation to the priesthood, and undertaking a parish placement as part of this process; book grants for ordinands; and financial support towards fees. Grants are also available for clergy engaged in post-ordination study.
www.cleaver.org.uk/

The Church of England **Pensions Board** has a section on the Church of England website with information about how clergy pensions work and how to get further advice. There is a Pensions Helpline, on 020 788 1802

or pensions@churchofengland.org, and you can also ask to speak to an Engagement Officer for information on support provided by your diocese.
www.churchofengland.org/more/pensions

The **Money Advice Service** is a government website giving free, impartial advice on money matters including dealing with different economic, health and relational situations.
www.moneyadviceservice.org.uk/en

The **State Pension Entitlement** website will help you to calculate your state pension entitlement at retirement.
www.gov.uk/state-pension-age

Turn2Us is a charitable service helping people access money available to them through welfare, benefits, grants and other help. It gives a wealth of information and provides its own direct grants to people with or connected to a professional background (including religious leaders), and to those who have experienced a recent life-changing event.
www.turn2us.org.uk/

The **Foundation of Edward Storey** can provide help, grants and accommodation or offer a number of services to those closely connected to the clergy of the Church of England.
http://edwardstorey.org.uk

Citizens Advice is the online help from the Citizens Advice Bureau and provides information on your rights covering a range of topics.
www.citizensadvice.org.uk/

The website of the **Ordinands' Association** lists several funds that can help ordinands in financial need, including the Church Times TAP Fund, CPAS, the Ellend Society, St Aidan's College Charity, the Anglo-Catholic Ordination Candidates Fund, the Leathersellers' Company, the Richards Trust and the Tim Burke Memorial Fund.
https://ordinands.wordpress.com/finance/financial-hardship/

There are also several charities that support clergy in a specific geographical area: ask your diocese for details of any in your locality.

> OUR PARISH SHARE IS AN AMAZINGLY PHILANTHROPIC MODEL, BASED ON ABILITY TO PAY.
>
> Male stipendiary minister, 2006

PARTICIPATION WELLBEING

Inclusive Church is a network of churches, groups and individuals uniting together around a shared vision of a church which celebrates and affirms every person and does not discriminate.
http://www.inclusive-church.org/

WATCH (Women and the Church) is a national organisation working actively for gender justice, equality and inclusion in the Church of England.
https://womenandthechurch.org/

THE CHURCH ASSUMES EVERYONE IS A PARISH PRIEST STILL, AND PAID PARISH PRIEST.

Female self-supporting minister and chaplain, 2011

AWESOME (Anglican Women Evangelicals: Supporting our Ordained Ministries) is a network of women ordained into the Anglican Church from across the evangelical spectrum. It includes all stages of ministry, from ordinands to those who are retired, and exists to support and pray for one another in ministry, learning from scripture, the Spirit and one another, and to give a voice to ordained evangelical women in the wider Church.
https://awesome.org.uk/

The role of the Church of England's **Committee for Minority Ethnic Anglican Concerns (CMEAC)** is to identify, monitor and take forward concerns of BAME Anglicans and make recommendations for change.
https://www.churchofengland.org/more/policy-and-thinking/our-views/race-and-ethnicity

AMEN (Anglican Minority Ethnic Network) is an independent group promoting the presence and participation of Minority Ethnic Anglicans in all structures of the Church of England in the service of the Gospel of Jesus Christ.
https://www.amenanglican.org.uk/home

Workplace Chaplaincy Mission UK (WCM UK) is a British network of over 500 practitioners engaged in workplace chaplaincy mission.
http://www.workchaplaincyuk.org.uk/

CHRISM is the national association for all Christians who see their secular employment as their primary Christian ministry and for those who support that vision.
http://chrism.org.uk/

OneBodyOneFaith is an ecumenical movement that wants to help churches and faith communities to have intelligent and compassionate conversations about sexuality, and wants individuals to be able to integrate their sexuality and spirituality in ways which are healthy and life-affirming.
http://onebodyonefaith.org.uk/

Living Out is an evangelical group helping churches and same-sex attracted Christians find a plausible way of living out a biblical perspective on sexuality.
https://www.livingout.org/

The main group in the Church of England which focusses on disability is the **Committee for the Ministry of and among Deaf and Disabled People (CMDDP).** You can contact the National Disability Advisor and the National Deaf Advisor through the CofE website.
https://www.churchofengland.org/more/church-resources/welcoming-disabled-people

THE ROMERO PRAYER

A Step Along the Way